MAKE SENSE OF: FOUCAULT'S PHILOSOPHY IN 60 MINUTES!

Del Moore

Copyright © 2022 Del Moore

"I'm no prophet. My job is making windows where there were once walls."

— MICHEL FOUCAULT

CONTENTS

1 POWER IS EVERYWHERE AND COMES FROM EVERYWHERE

On the 15th of October, 1926, Foucault was born in Poitiers, France and humankind would never be the same. He was a talented student who struggled with both mental illness and his sexuality throughout his entire life, as well as an authentic bon viveur until his late 20s. Despite the difficulties, during the 1960s, he established himself as an academic, holding several positions at French universities before being elected to the ultra-prestigious Collège de France in 1969, where he served as Professor of the *History of Systems of Thought* until his death, in 1984.

What a peculiar name for a course, right?

Well, that position had to be coined mainly because of the unique character of Foucault's work, which crosses fields like philosophy, history, and politics. Foucault was a child of his time, a captivating personality that dedicated his career to dissecting the authority of the modern bourgeois capitalist state, including its police, courts, jails, doctors, and psychiatrists. He was fascinated with the concepts of power and social transformation and he focused on how these issues played out historically in the formation of our society.

We tend to oversimplify this transformation, he believed, by seeing it as a continual and inevitable pursuit of "freedom" and "reason." He claimed that as a result, we have a misunderstanding of how power works in modern cultures. To grasp the importance of such a statement let's take a look at the following picture, which summarizes some of the key concepts of his philosophically groundbreaking work:

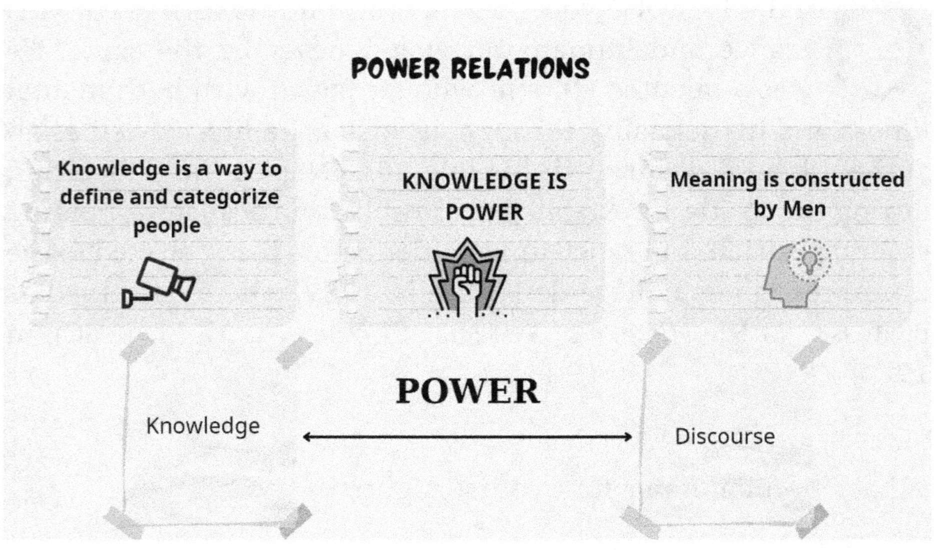

One of Foucault's main points is that power mechanisms generate numerous types of knowledge that gather information about people's lives. Thus, the exercise of power is supported by a framework of knowledge that dominates our society and in certain cases, it promotes the interests and power of some people while marginalizing others. In practice, this frequently justifies maltreatment of others in the name of correcting or assisting them.

So, Foucault challenges two important philosophical concepts of the time: The nature of truth and power. To put it in perspective, imagine a state that suddenly enacts a law forcing people with red hair into prison. Let's just say that this decision was based on recent research which suggested that red hair was a key factor in spreading a particular kind of disease. The law was supported by the vast majority of people and soon became official.

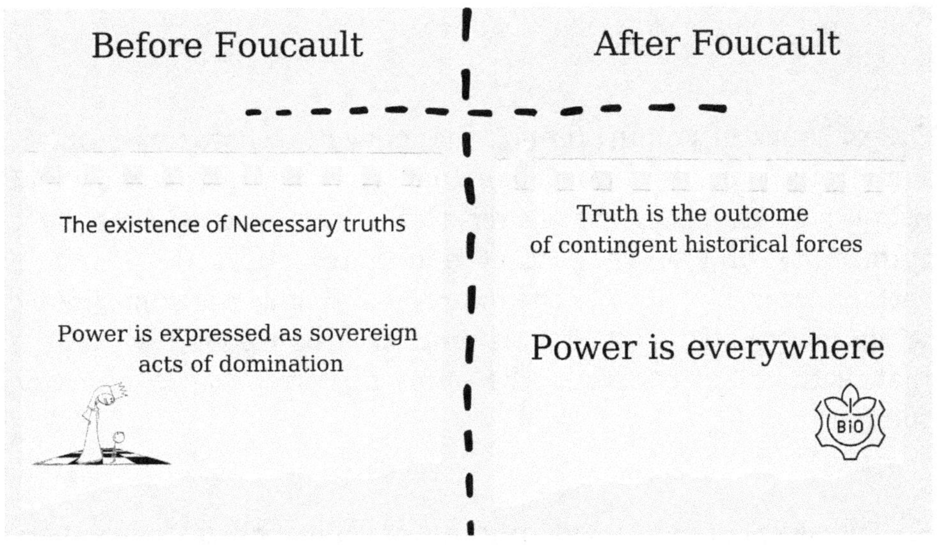

The typical interpretation of the above (quite far-fetched) example would be that power is to be located in the gulfs of the State, as it's believed to be a classical agent of sovereignty and thus the official structure which was historically proven to enforce its will upon its subjects. But if someone digs a bit deeper they will shortly realize that there are multiple agents involved in this situation. Foucault would ask in particular:

1. What is the role of the scientists who were deemed as the ones responsible for explaining the world around us?

2. Are people themselves to be accounted for legitimizing the law?

3. What is the relationship between the official data provided (Knowledge) and the agents who willingly sacrificed their fellow citizens based on the truth proceeding from the scientific 'facts'?

Just think about the above questions for a while and expand: Who legitimized whose power? Is power linear, coming one way from a specific centralized structure, or does it seem to create several sideways across the body of our society?

Don't sweat it too much though because Foucault himself seems to be pretty clear about it:

"Power is everywhere and comes from everywhere"

And yes, you may have realized by now that Michel wasn't exactly the life and soul of the party. But take the moment to realize the important insights he offered to our perception of the world and society. Foucault is one of the few thinkers who recognized that power is in constant flux, penetrating our interpersonal relationships (at any given moment) but at the same time, he is probably one of the less few who suggested that power may be a necessary, creative, and good force in society, rather than only a negative, coercive, or oppressive one that pushes us to do things against our will:

"We must cease once and for all to describe the effects of power in negative terms: it 'excludes', it 'represses', it 'censors', it 'abstracts', it 'masks', it 'conceals'. In fact power produces; it produces reality; it produces domains of objects and rituals of truth. The individual and the knowledge that may be gained of him belong to this production"

Again, based on the example with the anti-red hair legislation you can see how power and knowledge seem able to make an explosive cocktail that produces factuality. By providing discipline and compliance to the people, even the most preposterous law can be part of the "regimes of truth". Drawing on this conception, instead of focusing on the traditional 'sovereign' and 'episodic' exercise of power used by feudal states to persuade their subjects, Foucault identified a new kind of 'disciplinary power' located in the administrative systems of the 18th century Europe.

At the last stages of his career, this "disciplinary power" transforms into the concept of biopolitics, another term that is inextricably related to Foucault's philosophy.

But enough for now.

Until this point, I've provided you with the most essential information concerning Foucault's concepts on power and knowledge (the core of his philosophy). But, of course, there is much more! In the chapters that follow we'll take it a step further, diving deep into his work, while trying to make sense of his theories as a whole.

To cut it short and make it as comprehensive as possible, each chapter will contain a summary of the core concepts along with several remarks which will give you an idea of how Foucault's theory can be implemented in everyday cases.

Remember that this book serves my personal view on extensive academic material and in no case does it include the wholeness of Foucault's theory. It should be used as a handbook for people who want to engage with philosophy in a fun and comprehensive way, or students who need to freshen up their knowledge on this subject.

2 WE ARE ALL MAD DOWN HERE

In *"History of Madness"* which was Foucault's first work and a product of his thesis, there is a trend outlined, which seemed to had spread across Europe of the 17th century, and saw the construction of institutions (asylum-like prisons) that secluded people who were labeled as 'irrational' (Foucault named this series of events as *"The Great Confinement"*). The problem was that not only were the insane included, but also the jobless, single mothers, heretics, prostitutes, and anybody else thought to be socially unproductive or disruptive.

Throughout the book, Foucault emphasizes that madness is a social construct that is dependent on the culture in which it exists. The way madness is understood and experienced in a particular culture is determined by a variety of cultural, intellectual, and economic systems, and society shapes its experience of madness accordingly.

 Madness was an experience that was incorporated into the rest of the world during the Renaissance, but it had been acknowledged as a moral and mental sickness by the nineteenth century.

 Western science and psychiatry are incapable of listening to the voices of the insane

 The alleged scientific impartiality was/is deployed for suppressing challenges to bourgeois morality.

Through a presentation of numerous historical accounts he manages to set the basis for his work by offering some interpretation of key-terms that are developed later in his theory. We've already mentioned on chapter 1 that Knowledge is power and Foucault seems worried about these shifting knowledge patterns that dictate humans' actions. He's also worried (as we'll see in the next chapter) about our understanding of history itself.

(!) These views are more apparent (but of course not exclusively) in totalitarian states. For example, plenty of sources have highlighted the brain-washing mechanisms that Kim Jong-Un uses on the people of North Korea to remain in Power. Can you imagine a better way of manipulating someone but convincing him that what they experience is normal?

(!) Chechnya is a dangerous place for LGBTQ people. Since 2017 there have been reports of several citizens getting detained, beaten, or killed because of their sexual preferences. In one of his most strikingly unreasonable moments, Chechen leader Ramzan Kadyrov denied that homosexuals even exist in his country. One can easily imagine that these views come along with a fairly familiar concept: Homosexuality is a sin, a practice that must be avoided and the culprits must be burned at the stake. Of course like someone would expect from any kind of authority, Kadyrov has an ax to grind and does that essentially in the same way as Kim Jong Un: by creating specific Knowledge structures which render an issue invisible.

So aren't we lucky that we happened to live far away from these jackasses? Well… Yes and No.

Foucault seems to believe that at least punishment is an honest act that inspires intense feelings and actions. People back in the middle ages were REALLY angry when a person was falsely accused and executed by the King in front of their eyes, which led to some of the first anti-authoritarian movements bursting against the elites. It was at the moment that authority concealed its existence, that fire seemed to wither and people stopped asking all the important questions.

(!) Now all things happen behind closed gates and thus, people are not able to experience the violence and cruelty of authority. You see the pattern here, right? It's the same creation of "visible invisibility" that was described in the case of North Korea & Chechnya. Foucault's point is relatively simple: If you don't experience "madness" don't expect to be able to resist the power that creates it for its benefit.

In this sense, every place is ruled by these fundamental principles of Power and Knowledge. It's a constant circle that feeds itself from the pain and misery of others. Take a walk downtown and you'll see a bunch of people living in the streets, starving and begging for a dollar or two. Is this civilization at its finest? Foucault suggests that we reflect for a while, at least before we start boasting about the things we've accomplished, and think: Is it possible that we are just pawns in the same structures that still exist (in only slightly different forms) since the dawn of history?

3 A NEW WAY OF INTERPRETING HISTORY

Archeology tries to examine the discursive traces and orders of the past in order to write a "history of the present".

Episteme (Science) is a just a set of discursive relations (as knowledge is too) and nothing more.

People living in previous ages had thought very differently but just as effectively.

We think of the west as the Mecca of civilization. The land of human rights that evolved through harsh times to spread the light of knowledge, science, and healthy politics to the rest of the world. To some extent (and by browsing just a bit through history) someone can get that this evolution happened on the backs of other nations but whatever, the fact is out there, plain and simple: We rock. We've got democratic systems of governance, a certain respect for different people, and an extensive legal background to deal with issues that may arise. So what is this guy bitching about?

Foucault clearly states that this logic is completely wrong and even an insult to our own ancestors (yes the same white Europeans that lived before us). You see, the view of history as constant progress that brings us closer to the "truth" is of liberal origins and had already been criticized A LOT during the 60s. At a time of political and social turbulence when people had to deal with the same power structures that kept dictating their lives all along (war, armies, police, authoritarian states) something seemed off. Most were thinking that either we are totally incapable of learning from history or someone keeps putting obstacles in front of us to never reach real progress, peace, and welfare.

Foucault actually agrees with both. First of all, he thinks that we are paraphrasing history. So to fix that, he invents the term *"archaeology"* which describes a method of looking at history as a way to understand the processes that led to what we are today. This is a history of knowledge that is mostly concerned with describing the change in the conditions that determine what counts as knowledge, instead of simply showing the transitions between different modes of knowledge.

For him, history had no purpose, and when it became clear that it was tangled in language, the question should no longer be what happened there, but most likely: how was it possible to make certain statements at that time? Surely we are historical subjects, with a past and a present, but for Foucault, all these events are completely random and organized through particular modes of knowledge that give them meaning. His work was to investigate under which circumstances that meaning comes up and why.

> **(!)** It's difficult to apply Archeology as a systematic approach to history and that's because (oh well) it is still difficult to figure out if Foucault provided a solid methodology at all. Still, this critical approach inspired others to re-evaluate history and approach it differently. In Edward Said's *Orientalism*, for example, the author suggested that the "Orient" was in fact a Western discourse formed for the purposes of dominating the East. The term which was widely accepted until the 19th and early 20th centuries as the study of Asian languages, history, and cultures ended up with negative connotations, as the reproduction of a series of stereotypes concerning the nations of the east (through the European lenses).

To offer that critique, a pure archaeological approach wouldn't be enough. It is one thing to compare and contrast the systems of thought that were employed in a particular era, and a whole other to evaluate the causes of the transition from one way of thinking to another. Foucault turned to Nietzsche for guidance and transformed his archeology into genealogy. But don't worry about the terms because he didn't bother to make a total distinction between these two and he keeps using the same methods for both kinds of analyses.

One thing to remember is that the point of a genealogical analysis is to show that a particular system of thought (which itself was discovered in its essential structures by archeology) was the result of accidental turns in history, not the result of rationally inevitable tendencies. As we'll see in the next chapter we seem to be living in world which is governed by laws but nothing has essentially changed. We haven't beaten inequalities nor we have created a peaceful society for all. And most importantly, as Foucault notes, we have no idea about the actual "nature" of power.

4 LIFE IS A PRISON

Discipline and Punish, written in the early 70's falls exactly between the *Archaeology of Knowledge* and the three-volume *"History of Sexuality"*, which can be understood as Foucault's journey from the formation of discourses to their impact. The interesting thing is that until that moment , Foucault did not seem concerned with power, but as the transition from archaeology to genealogy began it allowed him to study these discourses in action, or (to use his categories) as they really were: "truth regimes".

VOIR- SAVOIR- POUVOIR: To see is to know is to have power. This is central to Foucault's conceptualizations so keep it handy.

The power and strategies of punishment are dependent on information that produce and classify people, and that knowledge draws its authority from certain power and dominance relationships.

The jail is part of a network that infiltrates and penetrates society.

In his work, Foucault claims that punishing a criminal on public display was not a spectacle of pain but of the king's concentrated power. Power was negative or prohibitive as long as it radiated outward from the ruler, but during the Enlightenment, a new sort of power emerged: not a negative power (what you shouldn't do) but a positive one that multiplied and spread throughout our society. A distinguishing aspect of contemporary authority (disciplinary control) is its preoccupation with what individuals have not done, that is, a person's failure to meet needed criteria.

(!) Foucault means that all of us whether "inspectors" or "convicts", are subjects to the anonymous supervision of a plethora of laws. These laws are both official (legislation) and unofficial (beliefs, traditions etc) and play the main role on what we'll finally become. Simply think of some parts of your life that are governed by these "hidden" rules. Maybe your career decisions were based on the expectations of others. Do you actually wear the things you love or is your wardrobe a repetitive pattern of the things you've got used to like?

(!) The perfect analogy that Foucault uses to convince us about the gradual transformation of power relations is Bentham's *Panopticon*. This is nothing more than a prison design in which each inmate is isolated and hidden from the others (in separate "cells") and is constantly visible to a monitor located in a central tower. Prison Guards practically can't observe each inmate; Nevertheless, they might at any time. Because convicts never know if they are being watched, they must act as though they are always being watched. As a consequence, control is achieved more through the possibility of internal monitoring of people under control than through real supervision or severe physical limits.

The Panopticon idea may be applied to any institution of disciplinary power, not only prisons. From schools and factories to hospitals and offices all around the world the politics of control seem attached to a very specific pattern: In knowing we control and in controlling we know. So the terms Power and Knowledge are uncovered as having pretty much the same goals.

(!) Once you are submitted to a hospital doctors will know everything about you. They will check your history records, conduct tests, prescribe you the necessary medication, etc. For Foucault, this is just another case that clearly shows the function of power: The examination as a process will tell us everything about a person and then the subject which has already started to transform into an object, will be forced to a particular behavior (a course of treatment). It may seem a bit odd at first but remember: Power shouldn't always be described as something negative.

To cut things short, genealogies are *"histories of the flesh,"* as opposed to histories of minds or concepts. They investigate the historical practices that make the body an object of tactics and power deployments.

Discipline and Punish had a vital influence because of its capacity to highlight the processes of subject creation that occur in modern prison facilities. The contemporary jail not only punishes by denying its inmates of their liberty, but it also categorizes them as delinquent subjects, persons with a dangerous, criminal disposition.

These categorizations functioned similarly during the Great Confinement, as explained in chapter 2 by promoting certain connotations of good or evil. And they will be expressed in the same way in "History of Sexuality", Foucault's landmark, a few years later. The objectified subject that emerges out of these constant social procedures reproduces power relations in several spheres of his life while being trapped in this nexus of power relationships that, sadly seems never-ending.

5 POLITICS OF THE BODY

Sexuality is a social construct and it used as a means of social control

It has evolved from a random sequence of power relationships and there is nothing natural (or unnatural) about it.

We live in the age of biopolitics, an era which gives power (and the ones who hold it) an administative role in our lives.

*H*istory of sexuality is probably the most well-known book by Michel Foucault. But regardless of what someone may infer from the title, he is not interested in sexuality itself so much as he is interested in how it ended up being an object for knowledge. So the main question is why, in the past few centuries, have we increasingly come to see our identity as bound up with our sexuality.

According to Foucault, contemporary management of sexuality matches modern control of criminality by making sex an object of scientific disciplines that simultaneously give knowledge and dominance over their targets. However, it becomes clear that the power linked with sexuality sciences has a second component. There is control exercised not just via other people's knowledge of persons, such as physicians' knowledge, but also through individuals' awareness of themselves. Individuals internalize the standards established by the sciences of sexuality and monitor themselves to comply with these norms.

(!) Sharing these thoughts in the age of sexual liberation was provoking. The central line of thought argued that we needed to free our genuine sexuality from the restrictive systems of power. This exact idea was challenged by Foucault, who demonstrated how our perceptions and experiences of sexuality are always the outcome of certain cultural traditions and power systems and could not exist independently. Because there was no true or natural sexuality to release, the quest to liberate our suppressed sexuality was essentially flawed.

In these three volumes, the most anticipated theory of power was systematically provided. We should not try to look for the center of power, or for the individuals, institutions, or classes that rule, but we should rather construct a "microphysics of power" that focuses on the multiple locations of power spread throughout a society: families, workplaces, and everyday practices. One has to analyze power relations from the bottom up and not from the top down and study the myriad ways in which the subjects themselves are constituted in these diverse but intersecting networks.

Apart from the final formulation of his theory, in the three volumes of History of sexuality comes the formation of a political concept that has since then evolved in the universe of philosophy and political theory. Foucault is quite brief and doesn't offer much about the idea of biopolitics, which first appears in Volume 1 of History of sexuality, but we can capture the general meaning.

Foucault starts by comparing it with sovereign power, which he defines as a sort of authority historically predicated on violence (The right of kings to murder the people who didn't obey them). It was primarily exercised by "deduction" (taking something away): the right to usurp a piece of the nation's riches, for example, by placing a tax on products, goods, and services, or by demanding a portion of the subjects' time, strength, and, eventually, life itself. The responsibility to conduct war on behalf of the sovereign, as well as the enforcement of the death sentence for going against someone's will, were the most obvious manifestations of such power.

However, Foucault contends that the West's power processes have experienced a fundamental alteration since the seventeenth century.The rationale of biopower differs substantially from that of sovereign power, not just in terms of its purposes, but also of its means. The rising relevance of standards at the cost of the legal system is a significant result of its growth. According to Foucault, the supremacy of biopower as the archetypal form of power indicates that we live in a society where the power of the law has given way to regulatory and corrective procedures based on scientific knowledge. Although biopower penetrates conventional forms of political power, it is mostly the authority of specialists and administrators.

(!) Briefly, biopower is a population-management technique that first arose in the late eighteenth century. If disciplinary power is concerned with teaching the acts of bodies, biopower is concerned with regulating a population's births, deaths, reproduction, and diseases. Foucault didn't get the chance to offer a complete theory about biopower and biopolitics but his approach is one of the most direct confrontations against modern political systems.

(!) The importance of medical professionals' interventions in the social administration systems during the Covid-19 pandemic was really important in cutting back the spread of the disease, internationally. But could that be also a real-life example that could justify Foucault's theory?

And even if it does, could you describe it as something good or bad?

7 WHERE SHOULD WE GO FROM HERE?

When we read Foucault there should be no explanations that are based on dualisms. Concepts and subjects emerge in a context of power relations that simply exist and are labeled according to the needs of the era and the people who exercise and internalize power. We could say that after Foucault, history is naked and its subjects as well. However, only by getting to know our weaknesses and limitations can we move forward and change the rules that bind us.

Life is a prison and our body is too. But sometimes we just willingly sign our freedom over to others, to avoid something or gain something else. We accept the authority of our parents or partners and we stand there blushing while our teacher scolds us, unable to react. The importance lies in recognizing and accepting the power structures of our everyday lives while being able to actively challenge the ones that suffocate us.

END

www.ingramcontent.com/pod-product-compliance
Lightning Source LLC
Chambersburg PA
CBHW051942150726
47999CB00006B/2336